MATCH ATTAX

ANNUAL 2024

CONTENTS

IT'S TIME TO KICK OFF!

Welcome to the official Match Attax Annual 2024 – your ultimate guide to the best of the year's football action! Get ready to witness the greatest players in European football, the best teams and the next generation of ultimate football stars. Plus, you can put your own skills to the test with thrilling footy puzzles and awesome activities.

What are you waiting for? It's time for kick-off!

EURO FOCUS ON ...
ENGLAND

The English top-flight is the most action-packed league in world football. Let's remind ourselves of the titanic battle for last season's title!

MANCHESTER CITY

While City sat patiently in second place for much of the season, Pep's men hit a ruthless winning run which saw them leapfrog Arsenal and retain the top-flight trophy for a third successive year. Their free-flowing football saw the likes of Jack Grealish and Erling Haaland devastate opposition defences in true style.

PRIZED PLAYER

KEVIN DE BRUYNE

While Erling Haaland took most of the goal-scoring headlines, it was the flying Belgian, Kevin De Bruyne, who proved that he's the king of assists once again. He tore through opposition midfields to create over 16 goals for his team, as well as hitting 7 goals himself!

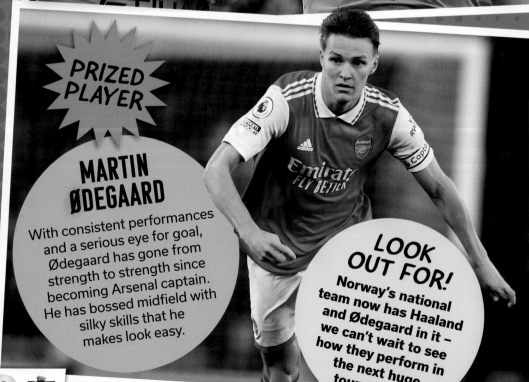

PRIZED PLAYER

MARTIN ØDEGAARD

With consistent performances and a serious eye for goal, Ødegaard has gone from strength to strength since becoming Arsenal captain. He has bossed midfield with silky skills that he makes look easy.

ARSENAL

The Gunners were the unexpected success story of the season! They took the league by storm and outplayed some huge clubs on their way to second place, only narrowly missing out on the title. With former player Mikel Arteta as manager, Arsenal are going to be contenders for years to come!

LOOK OUT FOR!

Norway's national team now has Haaland and Ødegaard in it – we can't wait to see how they perform in the next huge tournament!

NEWCASTLE

No one expected Newcastle to finish in the top four this season, but their energetic performances under manager Eddie Howe have seen them go from strength to strength. With a perfect mix of seasoned pros and hungry new talent, they are building something very special in Tyneside!

PRIZED PLAYER

ALEXSANDER ISAK

This season, Isak has announced himself as one of the hottest strikers in the English top-flight. Sure, he scores close to a goal every other match, but it's his style of play and touch of class that excites fans the most!

MANCHESTER UNITED

The red side of Manchester continued their rebuilding under manager Erik ten Hag with a solid campaign. Securing a top-four finish was important, but fans were happy to see their tactical game much improved. After years failing to mount a title challenge, United are showing signs of consistency – bossing teams and collecting points for fun!

PRIZED PLAYER

MARCUS RASHFORD

After a tough campaign in the previous season, Rashford returned to the form he is famous for. He bagged awesome goals against Manchester City and Barcelona in key matches, and went on to score an impressive 17 goals over the season!

LIVERPOOL

The Reds had a mixed season, with plenty of poor results leaving them in mid-table. A fine return to form for the team, led by club legend Mo Salah, saw them climb back up and finish just outside the top four places.

BRIGHTON

The Seagulls were one of the surprises of the season! After losing former manager Graham Potter last summer they hit their opponents with fast-paced tactics and attacking formations, including World Cup-winner Mac Allister!

ASTON VILLA

A poor start to the season saw Villa score just 7 goals in 11 matches and led to a change of manager. Enter Unai Emery, who led them from the bottom half of the table to finish in 7th place, scoring loads of goals and qualifying for the Europa Conference League!

EAM TALK

START

FINISH

START

ANSWER ON PAGE 68

MISMATCH ATTAX!

Have a look at these Match Attax cards featuring Joshua Kimmich. If you zoom in, can you spot five sneaky differences between the two?

MAN OF THE MATCH

MIDFIELDER

DEFENCE
95

VALUE
£11.5M

ATTACK
76

MAN OF THE MATCH

MIDFIELDER

DEFENCE
95

VALUE
£11.5M

ATTACK
76

Colour in a ball every time you spot a difference!

ANSWERS ON PAGE 68

9

PLAYERS OF THE YEAR

Check out the hottest heroes of the year and why they're the best of the best!

ROBERT LEWANDOWSKI
Striker • Barcelona + Poland

Lewandowski switched to Barca from Bayern Munich ahead of 2022–23 – and he smashed it from day one! The super striker showed off all of his goal powers, netting 23 in the league to take Barcelona to the title ahead of rivals Real Madrid. Lewy is a lethal scoring machine!

Champions League titles: 1
Spanish league titles: 1

GOAL GREAT: Last season Lewandowski scored his 600th career goal.

KYLIAN MBAPPÉ
Forward • Paris Saint-Germain + France

Watching Mbappé work his magic is pure entertainment! At PSG, he was so good that he even outshone the greats of Messi and Neymar. In 2022–23, the speedy forward scored 28 league goals as the French giants stormed to success. Give him the ball and Mbappé will do the rest!

Champions League titles: 0
French league titles: 6

VINÍCIUS JÚNIOR

Forward • Real Madrid + Brazil

Dribbling, crossing, assisting, scoring … Vinicius does it all with class and style at Real Madrid. The Brazil international is electric in possession and loves tricking and dazzling his way past defenders, as well as being a threat inside the box. In 2022–23 he made over 19 goal contributions in the Spanish league.

Champions League titles: 1
Spanish league titles: 2

JAMAL MUSIALA

Midfielder • Bayern Munich + Germany

Musiala is no longer just a hot young prospect with the talent to make a big impact in Europe – he's now the real deal and Bayern Munich's big star! You can't ignore his huge numbers, scoring 11 times and chipping in with a cool 10 assists. He might be young, but he's like a superhero in Germany!

Champions League titles: 0
German league titles: 3

TOTAL BALLERS

SUPER SAVERS

It takes immense skills, strength and confidence to be rated a top goalkeeper. Check out how these four are flying high!

GIANLUIGI DONNARUMMA

Club: Paris Saint-Germain
Top skills: Strength, agility, coolness

DONN DEAL
PSG have loads of cash, but they signed Donnarumma for free from AC Milan. Great business!

PSG are packed with attacking heroes, but between the posts they have another megastar! Italy ace Donnarumma is like a brick wall in defence – getting past this towering keeper is never easy!

UNAI SIMÓN

Club: Athletic Bilbao
Top skills: Agility, distribution, penalty saving

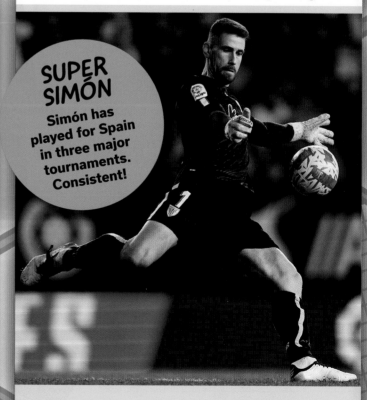

SUPER SIMÓN
Simón has played for Spain in three major tournaments. Consistent!

With his gloves or his boots, Simón is such a commanding character in the Spanish league. He reaches anything and everything that comes his way, plus he's confident playing out from the back!

THIBAUT COURTOIS

Club: Real Madrid
Top skills: Reflexes, catching, clearing

Courtois just keeps pulling out the stops, saves, blocks and catches to rack up his Real trophy count! His height, strength and rapid reflexes make him tough to beat at the back. He's a Bernabeu legend.

CITY SWITCH

Earlier in his career, Courtois won the league with Real Madrid's city rivals Atlético Madrid!

DIOGO COSTA

Club: Porto
Top skills: Concentration, energy, positioning

Costa has become one of Europe's most prized goalkeeping talents. All the big Champions League clubs love his reflex saves, coolness in one-on-ones and how well he quickly distributes the ball to get it forward. The Portugal stopper is going places!

PENALTY POWER

Costa saved three penalties in a row in the 2022–23 UEFA Champions League!

EURO FOCUS ON ...
GERMANY

The superstars from Bayern, Dortmund and Leipzig delivered another exciting season in the awesome German top flight. The title was a tough battle!

BAYERN MUNICH

Bayern were champions by eight points in 2022, but in 2023 it was much closer. Borussia Dortmund, Union Berlin and RB Leipzig gave them a fright! Jamal Musiala had his best season and Joshua Kimmich, Eric Choupo-Moting, Serge Gnabry and Leroy Sane chipped in with key goals and assists.

PRIZED PLAYER

JAMAL MUSIALA

Musiala's stats are huge, grabbing over 20 goals and assists combined. He's an attacking midfielder who finishes like a world-class forward with serious strong playmaker qualities, too.

RB LEIPZIG

PRIZED PLAYER

CHRISTOPHER NKUNKU

Nkunku was a wonderful weapon in Leipzig's forward line. In counter-attacks, wing play and pressing the opposition he was top class, plus his free-kick and penalty technique was eye-catching!

Leipzig kept up their record of always finishing in the top six since their top-flight debut in 2016–17. They came 3rd last season. Creative stars shone again with Christopher Nkunku, Andre Silva, Dominik Szoboszlai and the returning Timo Werner sharing the goals. Boss Marco Rose took over in September 2022.

BORUSSIA DORTMUND

Dortmund battled hard but fell short in their quest for a first title since 2012. Nico Schlotterbeck shone as Dortmund's chief defender, youngsters Jude Bellingham and Karim Adeyemi sparkled in midfield and Julian Brandt and Youssoufa Moukoko were lively in attack. Defeats to Werder Bremen, Leipzig, Cologne and Union were costly.

PRIZED PLAYER

JUDE BELLINGHAM

Goals, assists and influential displays came week after week. The England hero's third season in Germany was his best yet, as he became the ultimate midfield enforcer!

UNION BERLIN

Union only reached the top league in 2019. In 2022–23 they caused the big clubs lots of problems, winning 17 games to secure a top-four finish. Manager Urs Fischer produced lots of top displays in the league as well as guiding the club to the knockout stage of the Europa League, beating Ajax along the way.

PRIZED PLAYER

DANILHO DOEKHI

In his first season at the club, Doekhi has helped Union Berlin to a top-four finish in the German top-flight league. His command of the back four allowed his team to finish the season with a +12 goal difference. What a boss!

FRANKFURT

New boy Randal Kolo Muani arrived from France and ripped it up in Germany! Eintracht finished 8th, with help from Muani's 14 league goals and some electric displays. He made nine assists in his opening 13 games!

SC FREIBURG

Freiburg enjoyed another fifth-place finish under their long-serving boss Christian Streich. Michael Gregoritsch and attacking midfielder Vincenzo Grifo were the goal threats, with Grifo very assured from the penalty spot.

WOLFSBURG

Niko Kovac's Wolfsburg were inconsistent in the league. They had a slow start but a six-game winning run, including back-to-back 6-0 and 5-0 wins that helped them finish in 7th place. Crowd fave Maximilan Arnold clocked his 300th league game.

KNOCKOUT KNOWLEDGE

Read the clues to work out the mystery teams. They all reached the knockout stage of the UEFA Champions League in 2023!

DOWN

1. German club in yellow and black (8, 8)
2. Italian team with seven European crowns, including 2007 and 2003 (2, 5)
3. This team from Milan are certainly inter-ested in winning trophies (5, 5)

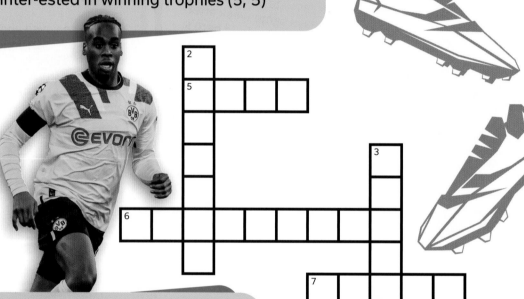

ACROSS

4. This team is always 'ready' in the Champions League (9)
5. This Manchester club made the final in 2022–23 (4)
6. Europa League winners in 2022 (9)
7. Portugal team, with four letters of that country in their name (5)
8. Benzema and Modric are legends here (4, 6)
9. Their home games are at the Diego Maradona Stadium (6)

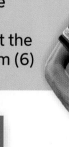

Topps
Match Attax

Topps

FOR

POWER
PLAY
85

VINI JR.
REAL MADRID

1

8.0M

DEFENCE
29

Attack
84

LIMITED EDITION

Topps

POWER PLAY

93

12.0ᴍ

FOR

ERLING HAALAND MANCHESTER CITY

2

DEFENCE

54

Attack

94

— LIMITED EDITION —

SHAPE SHIFT PUZZLE

Two of these outline shapes do not match the rest. Take a close look at the action and circle which two are slightly different!

NEXT GEN

YOUSSOUFA MOUKOKO

There has been hype around Moukoko ever since he broke into the Dortmund first team and bagged his first goal at just 16 years old. Youssoufa has it all – speed, power and accuracy!

KEY STATS

POSITION: Striker

CLUB: Borussia Dortmund

BORN: 20 November, 2004

SEASON	GAMES	GOALS
21–22	22	2
22–23	25	7

ALEJANDRO GARNACHO

Manchester United fans are on the edge of their seats when teenage hero Garnacho gets the ball. Dynamic and dazzling, his injury-time winner against Fulham last season was his first in the league since joining from Atletico Madrid!

KEY STATS

POSITION: Winger

CLUB: Manchester United

BORN: 1 July, 2004

SEASON	GAMES	GOALS
21–22	3	0
22–23	17	3

REAL DEAL: Garnacho opened his European account in 2022–23 by scoring the winner at Real Sociedad!

RICO LEWIS

Boss Pep Guardiola gives such high praise to the energetic play of Lewis. He can influence games from the start or as a super sub, and is an awesome right-back with the intelligence to raid midfield, too!

KEY STATS

POSITION: Defender/midfielder

CLUB: Manchester City

BORN: 21 November, 2004

SEASON	GAMES	GOALS
21–22	1	0
22–23	13	0

ALEJANDRO BALDE

Attacking full-backs who tackle, sprint and assist are vital to teams who play counter-attacking footy. Balde does all that, plus he learned loads from Jordi Alba, a legendary left-back at Barcelona!

KEY STATS

POSITION: Defender

CLUB: Barcelona

BORN: 18 October, 2003

SEASON	GAMES	GOALS
21–22	7	0
22–23	32	1

QUIZ

WORLD-CLASS WOMEN

See how much you know about the slickest female footballers!

1 Leah Williamson, Kim Little and Beth Mead are all connected to which club?

A. Chelsea ☐

B. Liverpool ☐

C. Arsenal ☐

2 Can you name the position Lucy Bronze usually plays?

A. Right-back ☐

B. Goalkeeper ☐

C. Striker ☐

3 How many goals did Georgia Stanway score in her first 21 matches for Bayern Munich?

A. 7 ☐

B. 6 ☐

C. 3 ☐

4 Midfield genius Keira Walsh made a big move to which European club in 2022?

A. Aston Villa ☐

B. Bayern Munich ☐

C. Barcelona ☐

5

Real Madrid's Caroline Weir plays for which Euro nation?

A. Wales

B. Scotland

C. Netherlands

6

In 2022–23, Alessia Russo, Ella Toone and Leah Galton all scored for ...

A. Manchester United

B. Tottenham

C. Manchester City

7

True or false? Chelsea legend Millie Bright plays as a winger.

A. True

B. False

8

Who became the all-time leading scorer in England's top league in 2020?

A. Ellen White

B. Fran Kirby

C. Vivianne Miedema

9

Manchester City ace Khadija Shaw is also known by what name?

A. Bunny

B. Rabbit

C. Cat

10

Skilful sisters Sam and Kristie Mewis have starred for which country?

A. Sweden

B. United States

C. Norway

ANSWERS ON PAGE 68

TOTAL BALLERS
EPIC DEFENDERS

When you're selecting your superstar team, which of these top-class defenders will you go for? These brilliant backline ballers have it all, keeping clean sheets for fun and building the base for their club's success!

DAVID ALABA

Club: Real Madrid
Top skills: Power, speed, intelligence

TITLE TRIUMPH
Alaba has won an unbelievable 11 league titles in his career. The last was in 2021–22!

Alaba won everything at Bayern Munich, then took his top-quality defensive skills to Real Madrid ... and bossed it there, too! The left-sided hero is so calm on the ball and powerful in tackling and blocking.

JOÃO CANCELO

Club: Manchester City
Top skills: Attacking, ball control, versatility

SUPER STATS
In his first 97 league games, Cancelo kept 41 clean sheets and made 16 goal contributions.

Surprised to see Cancelo ranked among the planet's top defenders? Don't be, because he's so good he could play in any defensive, or even midfield, role! The Portugal star is clever, fast, strong and such a fantastic team player.

VIRGIL VAN DIJK

Club: Liverpool
Top skills: Positioning, heading, leadership

Liverpool may not have been so dominant in 2022–23, but Van Dijk's influence and command at the back never dipped. If he ever misses a game, the Reds always struggle to replace his natural defensive ability. Rock solid!

BARGAIN BUY

Van Dijk cost Liverpool £75 million in 2017–18, but that now looks like an absolute steal!

RAPHAËL VARANE

Club: Manchester United
Top skills: Tackling, ball retention, communication

Varane came to Old Trafford in 2021 as a true champion with stacks of trophies and big-game experience. He only just turned 30 in 2023 and gets better every season, giving such confidence to United's defence!

EURO HERO

Varane first starred in the UEFA Champions League when he was only 18 years old!

DREAM TEAM TEST

Letters are missing from the shirts of this UEFA Champions League Dream Team. Fill in the gaps to complete each awesome player!

R__MS____E
1
GK

__ARQ__IN___S
5
CB

RUD__G___
22
CB

W_____ER
2
RB

S___W
23
LB

H___DER__O__
14
CM

R___RI
16
DM

___J___G
21
CM

___YMA__
10
RF

BE__Z___A
9
CF

V___ICI__S
20
LF

ANSWERS ON PAGE 69

GRID GOALS!

If you place the missing symbols in each grid, you'll score a goal! Complete every row, column and mini-grid so that each symbol only appears once in each!

1 DIFFICULTY: CLOSE-RANGE TAP-IN!

2 DIFFICULTY: SKILLED FREE KICK!

SYMBOLS

3 DIFFICULTY: SHOT FROM DISTANCE!

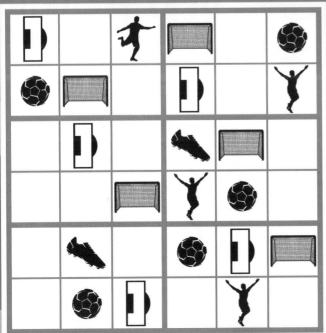

SYMBOLS

ANSWERS ON PAGE 69

EURO FOCUS ON ...

SPAIN

As always, the Spanish top flight delivered a stack of superstar players and performances. Barcelona capped an impressive season with the league trophy!

BARCELONA

In control of the title race for most of the season, Barca finished 11 points ahead of rivals Real Madrid to land their first league crown in four years. They lost just one of their opening 22 league games and recovered from losing to Manchester United in the Europa League to dominate in Spain. Boss Xavi was thrilled!

PRIZED PLAYER

ROBERT LEWANDOWSKI

Goalkeeper Andre ter Stegen kept 18 clean sheets in the league, but striker Lewandowski lit up the Nou Camp in his first season. He scored 23 goals to take Spain's golden boot and land the 12th championship of his career.

PRIZED PLAYER

VINICIUS

Vinicius was on fire in 2022–23. The Brazil star was too hot for defenders as he danced and dribbled to the box, putting keepers in a daze. Finishing solo strikes or slotting home sweeping team moves – Vini ruled!

REAL MADRID

Carlo Ancelotti's classy side didn't do much wrong, but chasing another UEFA Champions League prize stretched their squad. Dropping points to Real Vallecano, Villarreal and Mallorca proved painful, even though Karim Benzema, Vinicius, Rodrygo and Federico Valverde smashed 80+ goals and assists combined!

ATLÉTICO MADRID

Atleti were not as settled and dangerous as in previous seasons, with Luis Suarez leaving, Joao Felix loaned out and Memphis Depay arriving. Alvaro Morata could be relied on for goals, often from the bench, and captain Koke alongside Rodrigo de Paul were creative in midfield. A 3rd place finish guaranteed Champions League action.

PRIZED PLAYER

ANTOINE GRIEZMANN

Griezmann was in inspired form and looked like the eye-catching hero who first arrived in 2014. The France forward assisted, scored and ran defenders ragged with his playmaker qualities. An icon for supporters.

REAL SOCIEDAD

Imanol Alguacil's Sociedad team enjoyed their run to the knockout stage of the Europa League, eventually losing to finalists Roma. Back home, two five-game winning runs helped keep them in the chase for Champions League footy and to claim a very decent finish in 4th place.

ALEXANDER SORLOTH

PRIZED PLAYER

The giant Norway striker was a smart loan signing in 2022–23. He scored regularly throughout the season and bullied defenders with his power and rocket-fuelled shooting. Super Sorloth ruled in Spain!

REAL BETIS

Another Spanish side defeated by Manchester United in Europe, Betis came 4th in 2022–23 to give them another crack against continental opposition. Borja Islesias, Guido Rodriguez, Alex Moreno and William Carvalho all shone.

VILLARREAL

Villarreal started very brightly, losing only once in seven league games. If it wasn't for four straight defeats in early 2023, their 5th place finish could have been upgraded to the top four. Forward Samuel Chukwueze was a key creator.

ATHLETIC BILBAO

Bilbao can be pleased with their 2022–23 efforts given their small budget, lack of transfer action and losing key midfielder Ander Herrera to injury. The Williams brothers, Nico and Inaki, chipped in with goals and assists throughout.

MIDFIELD MARVELS

Mastering the middle of the pitch needs a range of skills, from strength and tidy passing to a switched-on attacking brain. So, meet four of the finest at their jobs!

GAVI

Club: Barcelona
Top skills: Touch, vision, movement

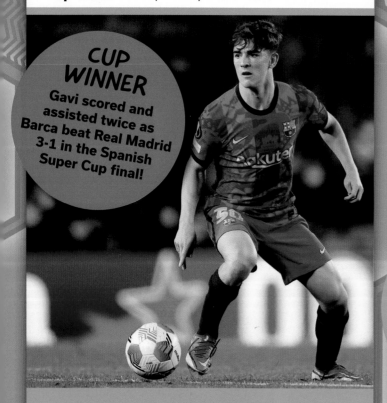

CUP WINNER
Gavi scored and assisted twice as Barca beat Real Madrid 3-1 in the Spanish Super Cup final!

Gavi only turned 19 in 2023 but he already bosses Barca's midfield. He's a livewire in central areas, rarely giving the ball away and always looking to release players in snappy forward moves. This guy is class!

CASEMIRO

Club: Manchester United
Top skills: Tackling, pressing, passing

CASE-WIN-O!
Casemiro won 11 of his opening 15 league games with Manchester United. What a winner!

Brazil baller Casemiro covers huge distances for Manchester United and patrols midfield with force and creativity. Spraying passes from deep, protecting his defenders and springing forward in attacks is what this guy loves!

JUDE BELLINGHAM

Club: Borussia Dortmund
Top skills: Footwork, creativity, stamina

Bellingham ripped it up for Dortmund in two elite seasons to become the hottest young player in Europe. Tall, athletic, composed and with laser-guided passing and shooting accuracy, it's no surprise he's been a breakout star in 2023!

BIG MOVE

Bellingham turned down English clubs, to prove himself abroad before taking on the English league.

JOSHUA KIMMICH

Club: Bayern Munich
Top skills: Energy, accuracy, passing

The German star has been one of the best at winning the ball and moving play into dangerous areas, but in recent seasons he's become a big assist maker too. Kimmich is already a great, and he's still getting better!

CORNER KING

Watch out for Kimmich assisting from his whipped corners – he's the best in the German league!

STADIUM SPOTLIGHT

Take a flying tour around some of Europe's most impressive stadiums!

TOTTENHAM HOTSPUR STADIUM

Club: Tottenham
Country: England
Capacity: 62,850
Opened: 2019

It's one of the coolest and slickest stadiums in the world! The construction is super high tech, and even the pitch can slide out so the arena is converted for concerts or big American Football games. Spurs fans love their new home!

SON STRIKES! Son Heung-Min scored the first league goal at the Tottenham Hotspur Stadium!

Club: England
Country: England
Capacity: 90,000
Opened: 2007

Wembley stages England internationals and major tournaments, plus exciting cup finals and even UEFA Champions League finals. It was re-opened in 2007 on the site of the famous old Wembley Stadium. A footy day out you'll never forget!

WEMBLEY STADIUM

NOU CAMP

DID YOU NOU? It's the biggest ground in Europe and previously held 120,000 spectators!

Club: Barcelona
Country: Spain
Capacity: 99,000
Opened: 1957

Whether you support Barcelona or not, every fan wants to visit the Nou Camp one day! The vast crowds, electric atmosphere and decades of amazing history combine for a unique experience. Barca, Barca, Barca!

MATCH ATTAX

ALLIANZ ARENA

Club: Bayern Munich
Country: Germany
Capacity: 75,000
Opened: 2005

The Allianz Arena literally lights up Munich! The clever design uses over 300,000 LED lights around the outside of the stadium – it changes colour and sparkles spectacularly for big league and UEFA Champions League encounters!

JUVENTUS STADIUM

Club: Juventus
Country: Italy
Capacity: 41,507
Opened: 2011

Juve's eye-catching arena is the most advanced in Italy. It's not the biggest, but with fans very close to the pitch and the noise of the crowd whipping around the stands, big European matchdays are super special!

METROPOLITANO

Club: Atlético Madrid
Country: Spain
Capacity: 68,000
Opened: 2017

An ultra-modern stadium and a stunning home for Atlético's stars, the Metropolitano has quickly built a reputation as a tough venue for away teams to get a win. Atlético legend Antoine Griezmann scored the first ever goal here!

CELTIC PARK

Club: Celtic
Country: Scotland
Capacity: 60,000
Opened: 1892

Celtic fans like to call their ground Paradise! Even though it's very old, Celtic Park's large capacity and the unique atmosphere generated here – especially in huge games against Rangers – makes it unlike any other footy home!

EURO FOCUS ON ...
SCOTLAND

Home to some of the most fierce rivalries in world football, the Scottish season saw the top two teams race to a huge lead – but only one could finish on top!

CELTIC

Winning their ninth title in the past 10 years, Celtic were once again a cut above the rest. Their free-flowing footy was lethal, thanks to three of the top assist kings in the league – Aaron Mooy, Jota and Matt O'Riley all hit double figures!

PRIZED PLAYER

KYOGO FURUHASHI

Hitting 27 league goals is a number most strikers can only dream of, but Furuhashi made it look easy. His heroics to help Celtic retain their crown saw him nominated for the Player of the Year award.

PRIZED PLAYER

BORNA BARIŠIĆ

A leader from left-back, Barišić marshalled the Rangers defence all season. He also pushed the whole team forward, offering creativity from wide positions and an impressive nine goal assists from his wand of a left foot.

RANGERS

The Gers may have been runners-up, some 17 points behind Celtic, but they finished the season some distance above the rest of the league. Assists from James Tavernier and goals from Antonio-Mirko Colak saw them finish second and qualify for Europe once again!

ABERDEEN

A third-place finish is a great result for the team who finished third from bottom the season before. Manager Barry Robson saw Bojan Miovski and Luis Lopes bag an impressive 16 goals each to secure their best finish in five seasons!

PRIZED PLAYER

KELL ROOS

The Dutch keeper made a serious case to be Aberdeen's number one goalie, earning the second most clean sheets in the league. Teams failed to score past him in 11 matches!

PRIZED PLAYER

LAWRENCE SHANKLAND

The star striker became Hearts' first player in over 20 years to score over 20 goals in all competitions. He finished with 22 goals, making him the second–best goalscorer of the season.

HEARTS

After narrowly failing to match their third-placed finish of last season, Hearts had another excellent campaign and qualified for Europe for the second season in a row. An amazing achievement considering they were only promoted three seasons ago!

HIBERNIAN

Hibs' season went down to the final fixture as they battled Hearts for European qualification. 11 goals from striker Kevin Nisbet and 11 clean sheets from David Marshall rounded off a successful campaign.

ST. MIRREN

St. Mirren finished the season in 6th position, which was a just reward for a heroic campaign. Star goalie Trevor Carson made 95 saves on his way to 10 clean sheets – an impressive stat. They'll aim to go one better next season!

MOTHERWELL

Star striker Kevin van Veen hit 25 goals in 38 appearances, as Motherwell finished the season in 7th place. They were the only team in the bottom half of the table with a positive goal difference, and avoided defeat in each of their last six matches!

EUROPA LEAGUE

The Europa League entertained fans all season long, with epic players, big teams and goals galore! Only one team could lift the trophy and finish the season on a high!

JUVENTUS

As three-time European Champions, Juventus know what it takes to make the final! A tense semi-final tie against Sevilla saw Juve narrowly miss out on this year's final. A struggling forward line averaged just over one goal per game (including two penalties) but didn't have enough firepower to book their place in the final. They'll be back to challenge again!

SEVILLA

The Europa League specialists were at it again and back in the final. They found goals hard to come by and scored seven fewer goals than their opponents, Roma – and the final was no different. Despite Sevilla's 67% posession, the two teams were level at 1–1 after extra time and it went to penalties. Gonzalo Montiel hit the winning penalty to clinch the trophy!

ROMA

Roma were propelled through the competition by star player Lorenzo Pellegrini. The midfielder had a tournament to remember, providing key goals and assists. It was back-to-back finals for Roma, who won the Europa Conference the season before. All that stood in the way of a historic win was Sevilla, and the final was an action-packed 90 minutes!

LEVERKUSEN

The German side is managed by Spanish legend Xabi Alonso, and made it to the semi-finals with style! Scoring an average of two goals every match, their passing accuracy and dominant possession gave their fans a European cup run to remember! Unfortunately, it came to an end after a narrow 1-0 loss over two legs to eventual winners Sevilla.

TOP FACTS
The numbers behind an incredible Europa League season!

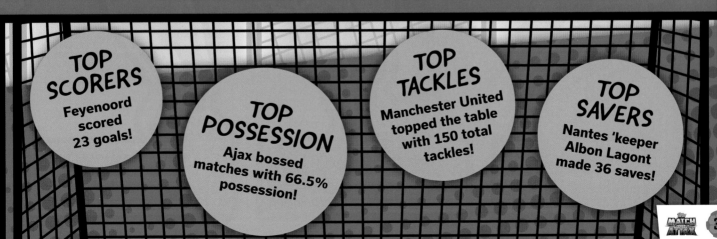

TOP SCORERS
Feyenoord scored 23 goals!

TOP POSSESSION
Ajax bossed matches with 66.5% possession!

TOP TACKLES
Manchester United topped the table with 150 total tackles!

TOP SAVERS
Nantes 'keeper Albon Lagont made 36 saves!

TROPHY CABINET

These brilliant players have won a stack of trophies in their careers.
Draw a line to link each player with their silverware stash!

**PAUL POGBA,
JUVENTUS**

**KEVIN DE BRUYNE,
MANCHESTER CITY**

**TRENT ALEXANDER-ARNOLD,
LIVERPOOL**

**RAPHINHA,
BARCELONA**

**MARCUS RASHFORD,
MANCHESTER UNITED**

**ANTOINE GRIEZMANN,
ATLETICO MADRID**

TROPHY COLLECTION 1

1 La Liga
1 Taça de Portugal
1 Taça da Liga

TROPHY COLLECTION 2

1 Europa League
1 FA Cup
1 League Cup

TROPHY COLLECTION 3

1 Europa League
1 League Cup
4 Serie A
1 World Cup
1 Nations League

TROPHY COLLECTION 4

1 World Cup
1 Nations League
1 UEFA Super Cup

TROPHY COLLECTION 5

4 Premier League
5 League Cup
1 FA Cup

TROPHY COLLECTION 6

1 Champions League
1 Premier League
1 FA Cup
1 League Cup
1 UEFA Super Cup
1 Club World Cup

RECORD-BREAKING ALVES

Brazil right-back Dani Alves, who has played for Barcelona, Juventus and PSG, has won more than 45 senior trophies in his incredible career!

ANSWERS ON PAGE 69

WOMEN'S CHAMPIONS LEAGUE

It was another thrilling season for the top European competition in women's football. Two English clubs made it as far as the semi-finals, but who eventually lifted the trophy?

BARCELONA

PLAYER OF THE TOURNAMENT: AITANA BONMATÍ
The Barca midfielder contributed an impressive 5 goals and 7 assists to help her team lift the trophy. She also covered almost 43 kilometres in distance!

Barcelona scored more goals in this year's competition than any other team. After a closely-matched semi-final tie against Chelsea, they eventually lifted the trophy after beating Wolfsburg in a frantic final that will be talked about for years!

WOLFSBURG

If you've got the tournament's top scorer playing for you, you've always got a chance. Ewa Pajor smashed in 8 important goals en route to the final, but the team couldn't topple Barca and finished as runners-up, losing just one match: the final. They'll be back challenging next season!

CHELSEA

The Blues were unlucky not to make it to the final after narrowly losing out 2-1 on aggregate to Barcelona in the semi-final. They dominated the early rounds, with assists from Guro Reiten and goals from star player Samantha Kerr!

ARSENAL

The Gunners were strong throughout the tournament but saw their journey come to an end after a tense semi-final against Wolfsburg. With a hungry young team full of creativity and hard work, they're sure to bounce back next season!

FAST FACTS

The stats behind a super season in the UEFA Women's Champions League!

GOALS
206 goals scored by all clubs!

TOP SPEED
32.4 kmh by Graham Hansen, Barcelona!

MOST FOULS
106 by Wolfsburg!

TOTAL SHOTS
248 by Barcelona!

DREAM TEAM

Can you find 11 legendary women's players in the grid below?
You've got five minutes until the final whistle –
tick off each one when you find them!

A	L	E	X	I	A	P	U	T	E	L	L	A	S
M	Y	P	K	A	L	E	D	F	Z	E	J	M	R
E	A	S	N	O	Y	I	B	C	N	N	V	P	A
D	T	R	B	P	W	N	E	O	O	A	L	P	C
E	G	C	Y	I	Q	L	O	F	R	O	D	O	H
I	S	K	B	E	W	T	R	Y	B	B	F	P	E
M	N	T	C	U	A	L	S	D	Y	E	P	A	L
E	L	A	O	L	T	R	N	E	C	R	H	R	D
N	U	J	L	S	F	B	P	O	U	D	T	D	A
N	C	E	B	W	V	H	I	S	L	O	K	N	L
A	F	N	P	O	U	M	Y	Q	B	R	S	A	Y
I	Z	E	R	Q	K	A	W	T	P	F	B	X	V
V	R	A	L	E	X	M	O	R	G	A	N	E	R
I	D	O	O	W	N	E	E	R	G	X	E	L	A
V	L	X	S	E	L	M	A	B	A	C	H	A	M

- [ ] MARY EARPS
- [ ] SELMA BACHA
- [ ] LUCY BRONZE
- [ ] RACHEL DALY
- [ ] ALEX GREENWOOD
- [ ] VIVIANNE MIEDEMA
- [ ] ELLA TOONE
- [ ] ALEX MORGAN
- [ ] LENA OBERDORF
- [ ] ALEXANDRA POPP
- [ ] ALEXIA PUTELLAS

ANSWERS ON PAGE 70

I FOUND THEM ALL IN____MINUTES!

CHRISTOPHER NKUNKU *RB LEIPZIG*

MID

POWER PLAY
88

8.5M

DEFENCE
71

Attack
86

LIMITED EDITION

Match Attax

Topps

CASEMIRO MANCHESTER UNITED

MID

POWER PLAY
85

8.5M

DEFENCE
86

ATTACK
66

1

LIMITED EDITION

NAME GAME

Fill in the missing name on each Match Attax card.
We've added quick clues to help you!

My initials are FV!

My first name is Leroy!

I rhyme with 'bed'!

My name contains the letters ESUSJ!

ANSWERS ON PAGE 70

45

CELEBRATION SPECIAL!

You've gotta know how to party on the pitch after bagging a cracking goal! Time to rate the famous goal celebrations of the superstars.

SCORE A SITTER!

Scoring is so easy for Erling Haaland – he can have a sit down afterwards! The Manchester City legend doesn't always celebrate with this relaxing routine, but when he does the fans think it's class!

MY RATING:

★ ★ ★ ★ ★

CHEF GNABRY

The Bayern Munich man celebrates his goals with a seriously 'tasty' tradition. Inspired by one of his favourite basketball stars, Gnabry pretends he is in the kitchen stirring a pot and cooking up something special for his team!

MY RATING:

★ ★ ★ ★ ★

DREAM-BÉLÉ

When Barcelona forward Ousmane Dembélé beats the keeper, his fave routine is pretending he's asleep! The rapid France ace has given defenders a proper nightmare with his speed and skills, though!

MY RATING:

★ ★ ★ ★ ★

KANE KISS

Tottenham hero Harry Kane gives out the kisses when he hits the net. Whether it's in the league or the Champions League, he sticks a smacker on his wedding ring finger as a lovely gesture to his wife. Sooo sweet!

MY RATING:

★ ★ ★ ★ ★

FLYING HIGH

Manchester City goal poacher Khadija Shaw enjoys flying like a plane when she scores for her team. After a goal-grabbing season, Shaw is jetting away to the clouds!

MY RATING:

★ ★ ★ ★ ★

KICK OFF

Over the years Roberto Firmino tucked away a range of quality strikes for Liverpool in big games. His most famous celebration was a karate-style kick high into the air. That explains why his team-mates didn't get too close!

MY RATING:

★ ★ ★ ★ ★

HEART HERO

Ángel Di María LOVES scoring – that's why he makes the heart shape with his hands when he fires into the net! Juventus fans share the love with their electric Argentine winger!

MY RATING:

★ ★ ★ ★ ★

GOAL GRABBERS

Having any of these goal machines in a team would be a total dream! They have smashed nets and frightened goalkeepers over the past 12 months and throughout their amazing careers. Read on to check out their stories and stats!

NEYMAR

Club: Paris Saint-Germain
Top skills: Footwork, shooting, speed

SUPER STATS
In 2022–23, Neymar reached 150 PSG games and his goal record stood at 109. Wow!

Neymar reached another level in 2023, clocking up a staggering 13 goals and 11 assists in the league. In the Champions League, he hit 5 goal contributions as the Brazil-liant forward keeps doing the business and showing off his powers for PSG!

LAUTARO MARTINEZ

Club: Inter Milan
Top skills: Finding space, link play, accurate strikes

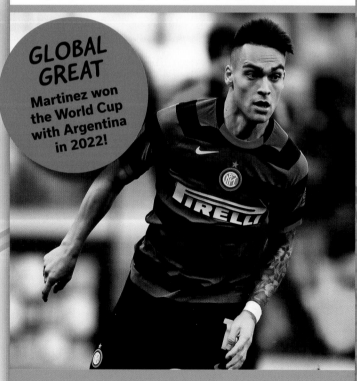

GLOBAL GREAT
Martinez won the World Cup with Argentina in 2022!

A regular scorer in the league and Champions League with Inter Milan, the energetic Argentinian star makes things happen in the final third. Defenders can't live with his classy movement, shooting and slick footwork!

HARRY KANE

Club: Tottenham
Top skills: Shooting, heading, creativity

Kane enjoyed another world-class season in front of goal. He became just the third player to reach the 200-goal mark in the English top-flight league, after Alan Shearer and Wayne Rooney, in an otherwise disappointing season for Spurs.

SPURS STAR

Kane became Tottenham's all-time leading goalscorer during the 2022–23 campaign!

CHRISTOPHER NKUNKU

Club: RB Leipzig
Top skills: Pace, dribbling, versatility

Crowned Player of the Year in the German league in 2022, Nkunku has kept improving and developing to become one of the finest attackers in Europe. He's a huge threat inside and outside the box and loves to assist his team-mates!

SUPER STATS

Nkunku grabbed 43 goals in his first 109 league games for RB Leipzig. Impressive – he doesn't play as a central striker!

QUIZ

GOAL MACHINES

How much do you know about the stars hitting the back of the net every week? Get your scoring boots on and test your super striker knowledge!

1 Who was the UEFA Champions League top scorer in 2022–23?

A. Raheem Sterling

B. Karim Benzema

C. Robert Lewandowski

D. Erling Haaland

2 In which year did Liverpool hero Mohamed Salah join the club?

A. 2012

B. 2017

C. 2018

D. 2021

3 If a player scores three goals in a game, what's this known as?

A. Triple trick

B. Hat-trick

C. Three trick

D. Goal trick

4 Who scored England's extra-time winner in the UEFA Women's Euro 2022 final?

A. Chloe Kelly

B. Beth Mead

C. Fran Kirby

D. Sarina Wiegman

GOAL LEGEND
With over 830 career goals, Cristiano Ronaldo is widely considered to be the best goal scorer ever!

5 When he played for Barcelona, how many seasons was Lionel Messi top scorer in La Liga?

A. 17

B. 10

C. 8

D. 2

6 Legendary striker Wayne Rooney scored 15 top-flight goals for which club?

A. Everton

B. Manchester United

C. Derby County

D. Fulham

7 In his first season with Manchester City, how many league goals did super striker Erling Haaland score in his first 31 matches?

A. 100

B. 20

C. 36

D. 10

8 Paris Saint-Germain star Kylian Mbappe wears which number for the club?

A. 17

B. 14

C. 7

D. 10

9 How many games did Harry Kane take to reach 100 Premier League goals?

A. 97

B. 112

C. 141

D. 189

10 Which FA WSL team does striker Vivianne Miedema play for?

A. Chelsea

B. Manchester City

C. Arsenal

D. Tottenham Hotspur

ANSWERS ON PAGE 70

UEFA CHAMPIONS LEAGUE

The biggest teams in Europe provided fans with a thrilling Champions League tournament. Four giants of football made it to the final four, but there could only be one winner in Istanbul!

INTER MILAN

Inter Milan may have an experienced team and a grand ageing stadium, but Inter are on the up! Making more tackles than any other team in the tournament, and beating their city rivals in the semi-final, saw them reach their first UEFA Champions League final in 13 years. The dream may have ended with defeat to Manchester City but they'll no doubt be back!

AC MILAN

AC Milan are a team with a rich history in the UEFA Champions League, winning the trophy an incredible seven times. They came agonisingly close to adding another but lost out to bitter city rivals Inter Milan in an epic semi-final tie. Their tournament highlight was surely beating Italian league champions Napoli 1-2 over two legs in a thrilling quarter-final clash!

REAL MADRID

No club has won the Champions League more than Real, with an impressive 14 titles to their name. Throughout this tournament, star man Vinicius Junior led their attacks with seven goals and six assists. After a dominant 4-0 aggregate score over Chelsea, Real had the trophy in their sights... but couldn't edge past Manchester City in an entertaining semi-final tie.

MANCHESTER CITY

After winning the English top-flight and the FA Cup, City were chasing an historic treble. Pep Guardiola's team made light work of Real Madrid in the semi-finals, and a slick goal from Rodri saw them lift the trophy over Inter Milan. It was a night to remember in Istanbul. City are Champions of Europe!

TOP STATS
Which players charged to the top of the rankings?

Man City's Erling Haaland scored 12 goals!

AC Milan's Sandro Tonali ran a total of 127.5 kilometres!

Bayern Munich's Alphonso Davies hit a top speed of 37.1 km/h!

Inter Milan's André Onana played 990 minutes of football!

NEXT GEN

MATHYS TEL

After captaining France to the Euro Under-17 crown, this exciting attacker moved from Rennes in France to German giants Bayern in 2022. At just 17 years and 126 days old he became the club's youngest ever goalscorer. He's going to be awesome!

KEY STATS

POSITION: Forward

CLUB: Bayern Munich

BORN: 27 April, 2005

SEASON	GAMES	GOALS
21-22	9	0
22-23	22	5

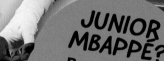

JUNIOR MBAPPÉ?
Because of his playing style, Tel has been compared to France forward Kylian Mbappé!

MOHAMED-ALI CHO

A teenage scorer in the French league before switching to Spain for 2022–23, this highly promising forward shows his strength, speed and attacking vision whenever he gets minutes with Real Sociedad. Cho's development will be very exciting!

KEY STATS

POSITION: Forward

CLUB: Real Sociedad

BORN: 19 January, 2004

SEASON	GAMES	GOALS
21-22	32	4
22-23	17	0

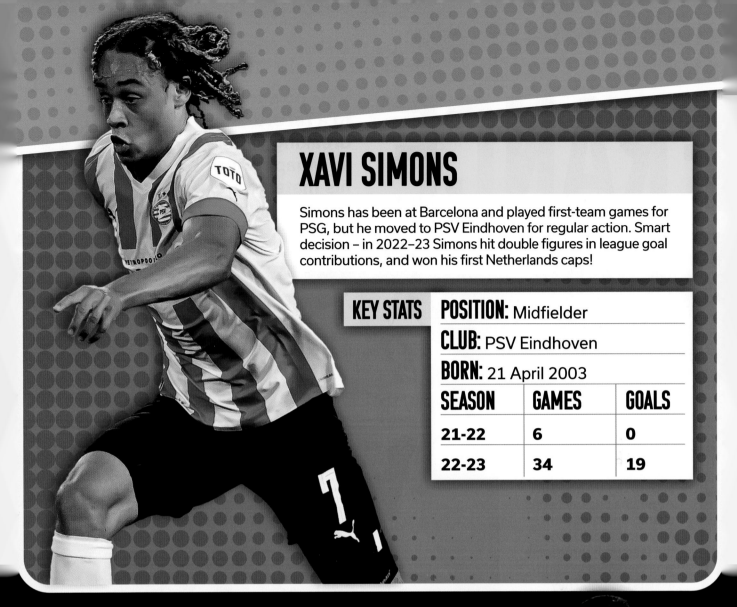

XAVI SIMONS

Simons has been at Barcelona and played first-team games for PSG, but he moved to PSV Eindhoven for regular action. Smart decision – in 2022–23 Simons hit double figures in league goal contributions, and won his first Netherlands caps!

KEY STATS

POSITION: Midfielder

CLUB: PSV Eindhoven

BORN: 21 April 2003

SEASON	GAMES	GOALS
21-22	6	0
22-23	34	19

ANTÓNIO SILVA

Silva hadn't even made a first-team appearance ahead of 2022–23, but he's already a highly prized young defender. Lots of Europe's major clubs are impressed with his solid and composed defending – he's on track for a BIG future!

KEY STATS

POSITION: Centre-back

CLUB: Benfica

BORN: 30 October, 2003

SEASON	GAMES	GOALS
21-22	0	0
22-23	30	3

EURO PRIZE
Silva won the UEFA Youth League with Benfica, beating RB Salzburg 6-0 in the final!

MATCH ATTAX

EURO FOCUS ON...
FRANCE

PSG powered to a record-breaking victory as Mbappé and his mates were unstoppable!

PARIS SAINT-GERMAIN

A record 11th top-flight title was never really in doubt as PSG kicked off with 16 unbeaten games in a row. Lionel Messi was superb before and after Argentina became world champions, and with Neymar buzzing too, the fearsome threesome smashed 56 goals and assists in total. They were totally dominant!

PRIZED PLAYER

KYLIAN MBAPPÉ

Mbappé broke the 200-goal mark for PSG to become the club's record scorer in 2023. With 28 goals in the league, he took the golden boot for the fifth time in a row. In the Champions League he bagged 7 in 8 games.

MARSEILLE

PRIZED PLAYER

NUNO TAVARES

Alexis Sánchez may have rediscovered some of his best form, but Tavares was athletic and powerful at left-back and wing-back. On loan from Arsenal, the pacey Portugal ace proved he's got loads in the locker, scoring 6 goals!

Marseille knocked PSG out of the French cup but they couldn't stop their title party. Third place was sealed with cracking goals from Alexis Sanchez, assists from Jonathan Clauss, and Valentin Rongier patrolling midfield. A disappointing early Champions League exit focused Marseille's attention on finishing third and qualifying for the UEFA Champions League!

MONACO

Powerhouse midfielder Aurelien Tchouameni joined Real Madrid in 2022, but luckily Wissam Ben Yedder and new boy Breel Embolo kept their scoring boots on as Monaco grabbed 6th spot in the table. Bayer Leverkusen dumped them out of Europe on penalties, but overall it was a pretty sweet season on the sunny south coast!

PRIZED PLAYER

WISSAM BEN YEDDER

Helped by the assists of Embolo and Aleksandr Golovin, Ben Yedder had a strong finish to the season with 18 goals in his final 6 games. The experienced captain was untouchable at times!

PRIZED PLAYER

LOIS OPENDA

The Belgium forward enjoyed being involved with 19 goals in 2022–23. His most memorable 90 minutes came against PSG in January, scoring and assisting with a cheeky backheel during a big 3–1 win!

LENS

Lens finished 2nd in the league with 84 points, an improvement on 7th place and 62 points the season before. Florian Sotoca, Lois Openda and Wesley Said kept defenders busy with their attacking moves, while Kevin Danso, Jonathan Gradit and Facundo Medina formed a tight unit at the back.

LILLE

The 2021 champions couldn't pull off another amazing season like two years ago, finishing 5th this time. Canada international forward Jonathan David was their hero once again, blasting 22 goals for the club.

RENNES

Mathys Tel, Kamaldeen Sulemana and Nayef Aguerd left either just before or during the season, but Martin Terrier, Amine Gouiri, Arnauld Kalimuendo and Benjamin Bourigeaud were all effective around the box to fire Rennes to 4th place.

NICE

Nicolas Pepe, Ross Barkley, Aaron Ramsey and Kasper Schmeichel moved to the south of France. Nice were stronger in the second half of the season, going 12 league games unbeaten and making the Europa Conference League quarter-finals.

PLAYERS OF THE YEAR

Discover more slick superstars and the stats & facts that make them the best!

ERLING HAALAND

Striker • Manchester City + Norway

Goals, goals, goals ... Haaland was sensational in his first season in England! He reached a ridiculous 36 league strikes during the campaign as Manchester City challenged Arsenal for the title. The scary thing is that Haaland will just keep improving – even two goalkeepers won't stop him!

Champions League titles: 1
English league titles: 1

HAT-TRICK HAALAND
Erling netted four hat-tricks in his first 19 league appearances!

LIONEL MESSI

Striker • PSG + Argentina

Messi turned 35 ahead of 2022–23 but showed no sign of stopping his epic scoring and assisting! In the Champions League he scored 4 more European goals and displayed all of his famous magic and skills. In the league he helped PSG race to another title. Messi is the ultimate attacker!

Champions League titles: 4
French league titles: 2

MARTIN ØDEGAARD

Midfielder • Arsenal + Norway

Ødegaard's incredible energy, vision and leadership from central midfield was the key ingredient in Arsenal's shock title charge. Without the all-action Norway star, The Gunners would not have been near the top of the league. The fans worship every blade of grass his brilliant boots touch!

Champions League titles: 0
English league titles: 0

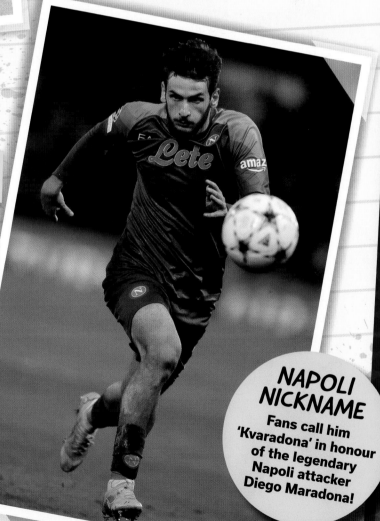

KHVICHA KVARATSKHELIA

Winger • Napoli + Georgia

Surprised to see Kvaratskhelia among these greats? Don't be, because his immense displays put Napoli on cruise control in the Italian league! The fantastic winger scored and assisted all season after arriving as an unknown in summer 2022. KK's value has rocketed from £9 million to £90 million!

Champions League titles: 0
Italian league titles: 1

NAPOLI NICKNAME

Fans call him 'Kvaradona' in honour of the legendary Napoli attacker Diego Maradona!

QUIZ

FOOTY FIGURES

How well do you know your numbers?
Can you get all ten of these teasers correct?
Just match a number to each question!

QUESTIONS

1 How many games are there in a Scottish top-flight season?

2 What shirt number do Mo Salah and Gabriel Martinelli wear for their clubs?

3 How old was Bruno Fernandes when he made his Manchester United debut?

4 Approximately how much did the UEFA 2022–23 Champions League winners receive as an extra winners' payment?

5 How many teams play in Germany's top league?

6

What is the capacity of Arsenal's Emirates Stadium?

7

Manchester United have scored the most top-flight league goals between 1992–93 and 2022–23. How many is it?

8

If a team plays with two wingers and two strikers, what formation could they be using?

9

How many games did Arsenal women's striker Vivianne Miedema play in to score 100 goals for the club in all competitions?

10

If a player scores a 'brace' in a match, how many goals is that?

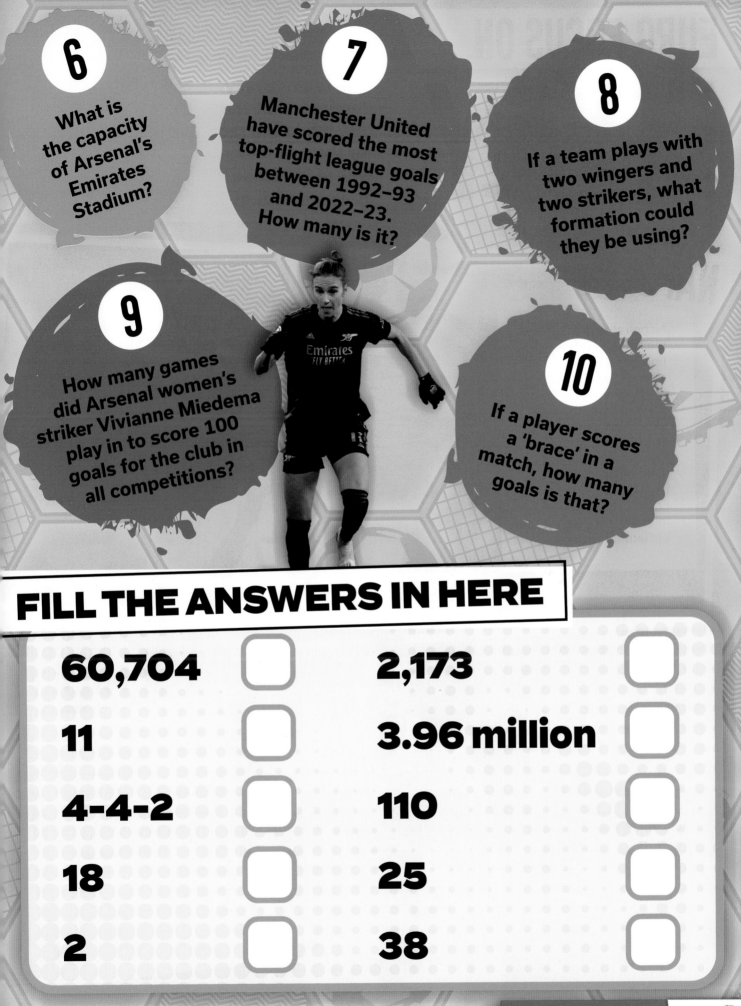

FILL THE ANSWERS IN HERE

60,704	☐	2,173	☐
11	☐	3.96 million	☐
4-4-2	☐	110	☐
18	☐	25	☐
2	☐	38	☐

ANSWERS ON PAGE 70

EURO FOCUS ON...
ITALY

One team totally dominated at the top, while the race for the top four was mega close and so exciting!

NAPOLI

Napoli stormed the league in style, finishing 18 points clear of Lazio in second place to win their first title since 1990. Napoli didn't lose a game until January, and with Victor Osimhen and Khvicha Kvaratskhelia smashing in goals and Stanislav Lobotka bossing midfield, they were brilliant all season!

PRIZED PLAYER

KHVICHA KVARATSKHELIA

The awesome winger reached double figures for goals and assists, giving defenders nightmares for 90 minutes! The Georgia star is fast, skillful, direct and deadly in the box.

INTER MILAN

PRIZED PLAYER

NICOLO BARELLA

Alongside Hakan Calhanoglu in midfield, Barella has been an attacking hero for Inter. In 2022-23 he was directly involved in 11 league goals and caused chaos for the opposition!

Four defeats in their opening eight league games did Inter too much damage as they chased Napoli at the top. Defender Alessandro Bastoni, Nicolo Barella in midfield and forward Lautaro Martinez were key stars. If striker Romelu Lukaku had stayed fit for longer, then their season could've been very different!

AC MILAN

Defending champs Milan slipped to a 4th placed finish. At the start of 2023, a seven-game winless run in all competitions bashed their confidence and they settled for securing Champions League footy for 2023–24. Defender Fikayo Tomori, striker Olivier Giroud and midfielder Sandro Tonali impressed.

PRIZED PLAYER

RAFAEL LEAO

Dribbling, shooting, crossing, speedy runs ... Leao does it all for AC Milan. Playing as a central forward or wide, the Portugal international races like a rocket and blasts the ball with laser accuracy!

ROMA

After winning the Europa Conference League and finishing sixth in 2022, Jose Mourinho's Roma came 6th in 2023. Their run to the final of the Europa League perhaps took their eye off the league race, but forwards Paulo Dybala, Tammy Abraham and Lorenzo Pellegrini were a constant source of goals.

PAULO DYBALA

Dybala joined from Juventus before the season, adding vast experience and cute attacking skills to Roma. His return of 11 goals and 6 assists shows what a clever signing he was by Mourinho.

PRIZED PLAYER

JUVENTUS

Juve had off-field problems and key players Federico Chiesa and Paul Pogba were troubled with injury. Dusan Vlahovic and Angel Di Maria looked sharp in attack, though, as the club scored 55 goals in the league!

LAZIO

Lazio only lost once in their first 11 league games to keep pace with the top four – eventually finishing 2nd. Captain Ciro Immobile scored his 190th league goal and heavy defeats, like a 3-0 loss to Juve, were rare.

ATALANTA

Atalanta impressed again by taking on Italy's biggest clubs with their stylish attacking play. They even managed to beat Salernitana 8-2! New winger Ademola Lookman was the star, bagging 18 league goals and assists combined.

UEFA EUROPA CONFERENCE LEAGUE

The third tier of European football has become a favourite with fans who want to see their teams take on some of Europe's finest players. What a year it was!

WEST HAM UNITED

The Irons went the entire season unbeaten in Europe, and reached their first European final in over 40 years. A tense match against Fiorentina looked liked it was going to extra time, until Lucas Paquetá put Jarrod Bowen through on goal – and the boyhood West Ham fan fired in a last-minute winner to clinch the trophy!

TOP SCORER
MICHAIL ANTONIO 6

TOP SCORER
VANGELIS PAVLIDIS 5

AZ ALKMAAR

The Dutch side caught the eye with accurate passing and energetic performances from their young squad. Packed with talent, they didn't lose at home until the semi-finals, but fell to West Ham just one match from the final. They won a lot of fans across the tournament who will hope to see them again!

FIORENTINA

The Italian side from Florence scored more goals than any other team (37) and hit over three goals in seven different matches! After losing the semi-final first leg, Fiorentina took Basel to extra time in the return leg, where they eventually triumphed 3-4. They were the best team for ball recoveries, making them difficult to break down – and in the final they narrowly missed out on lifitng the trophy, conceding a last-minute goal.

TOP SCORER
ARTHUR CABRAL 7

TOP SCORER
ZEKI AMDOUNI 7

BASEL

The Swiss side has played in Europe more than any other Swiss team – and all their experience was on show as they made it to the semi-final. They drew more matches than any other team, but finally missed out on the trophy after a close loss to Fiorentina. After conceding way more goals than any other side in the tournament, they'll be looking to improve their defence ahead of next season.

DID YOU KNOW?
There was one goal scored every 34 minutes throughout this year's UEFA Europa Conference League!

WOMEN'S TOP-FLIGHT LEAGUE

The women's league is full of superstars and incredible goals, which is why it is selling out stadiums across the country. Let's take a look at this year's action!

CHELSEA

Chelsea topped the table to win their fourth title in a row. Goals from player-of-the-year Sam Kerr saw them win the FA Cup and only just miss out on an historic treble, losing the league cup final to Arsenal!

MANCHESTER UNITED

The Red Devils pushed Chelsea all the way this season and came so close to taking the title back to Manchester. Their strikers may have got the goals, but 'keeper Mary Earps and defender Ona Batlle kept an amazing 11 clean sheets in their first 20 matches!

ARSENAL

The Gunners had another great year of footy. Star striker Stina Blackstenius bagged 15 league goals to lead them to a top–four finish. They also won an impressive sixth league cup final trophy, beating Chelsea 3-1 to lift their first silverware in four seasons!

MANCHESTER CITY

City had a solid campaign and managed to finish in the top four, making it eight seasons in a row they've done so. Striker Khadija Shaw was the star of the show, with 25 goals in all competitions, including one in a 6-2 demolition of West Ham!

WSL 2022-23 WONDER STATS!

The greatest stats from a great women's season!

BIGGEST HOME WIN
Chelsea 7-0 Everton

HIGHEST SCORING GAME
West Ham 4-5 Brighton

HIGHEST ATTENDANCE
47,367 at Arsenal vs Tottenham

BEST GOAL DIFFERENCE
+42 (Manchester United and Chelsea)

TOP SCORER
Aston Villa's Rachel Daly scored 20 goals

ANSWERS

PAGE 8: TEAM TALK

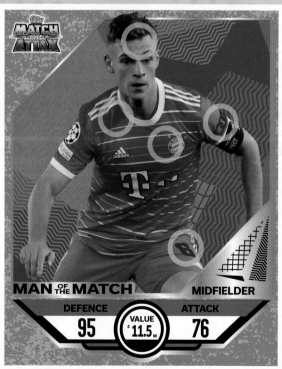

PAGE 9: MISMATCH ATTAX!

PAGE 16: KNOCKOUT KNOWLEDGE

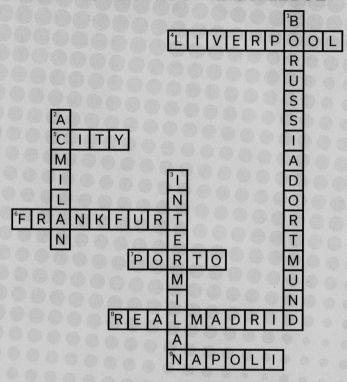

PAGE 19: SHAPE SHIFT PUZZLE

6   10

PAGES 22-23: QUIZ: WORLD-CLASS WOMEN PUZZLE

1 – **C:** Arsenal
2 – **A:** Right-back
3 – **B:** 6
4 – **C:** Barcelona
5 – **B:** Scotland
6 – **A:** Manchester United
7 – **B:** False
8 – **C:** Vivianne Miedema
9 – **A:** Bunny
10 – **B:** United States

PAGE 26: DREAM TEAM TEST

RAMSDALE
1
GK

MARQUINHOS
5
CB

RUDIGER
22
CB

WALKER
2
RB

SHAW
23
LB

HENDERSON
14
CM

RODRI
16
DM

DEJONG
21
CM

NEYMAR
10
RF

BENZEMA
9
CF

VINICIUS
20
LF

PAGE 27: GRID GOALS!

PAGES 38–39: TROPHY CABINET

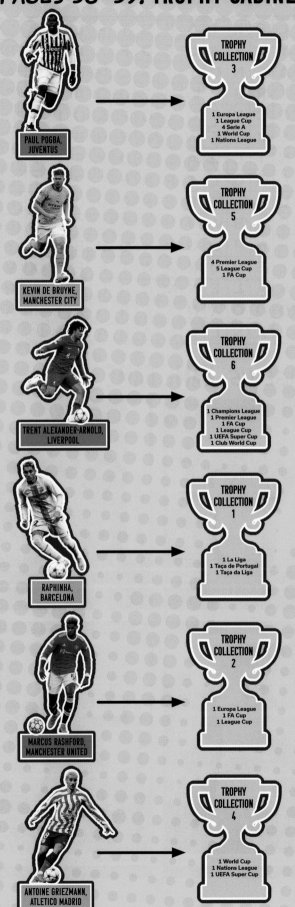

PAUL POGBA, JUVENTUS → **TROPHY COLLECTION 3**
1 Europa League
1 League Cup
4 Serie A
1 World Cup
1 Nations League

KEVIN DE BRUYNE, MANCHESTER CITY → **TROPHY COLLECTION 5**
4 Premier League
5 League Cup
1 FA Cup

TRENT ALEXANDER-ARNOLD, LIVERPOOL → **TROPHY COLLECTION 6**
1 Champions League
1 Premier League
1 FA Cup
1 League Cup
1 UEFA Super Cup
1 Club World Cup

RAPHINHA, BARCELONA → **TROPHY COLLECTION 1**
1 La Liga
1 Taça de Portugal
1 Taça da Liga

MARCUS RASHFORD, MANCHESTER UNITED → **TROPHY COLLECTION 2**
1 Europa League
1 FA Cup
1 League Cup

ANTOINE GRIEZMANN, ATLETICO MADRID → **TROPHY COLLECTION 4**
1 World Cup
1 Nations League
1 UEFA Super Cup

A	L	E	X	I	A	P	U	T	E	L	L	A	S
M	Y	P	K	A	L	E	D	F	Z	E	J	M	R
E	A	S	N	O	Y	I	B	C	N	N	V	P	A
D	T	R	B	P	W	N	E	O	O	A	L	P	C
E	G	C	Y	I	Q	L	O	F	R	O	D	O	H
I	S	K	B	E	W	T	R	Y	B	B	F	P	E
M	N	T	C	U	A	L	S	D	Y	E	P	A	L
E	L	A	O	L	T	R	N	E	C	R	H	R	D
N	U	J	L	S	F	B	P	O	U	D	T	D	A
N	C	E	B	W	V	H	I	S	L	O	K	N	L
A	F	N	P	O	U	M	Y	Q	B	R	S	A	Y
I	Z	E	R	Q	K	A	W	T	P	F	B	X	V
V	R	A	L	E	X	M	O	R	G	A	N	E	R
I	D	O	O	W	N	E	E	R	G	X	E	L	A
V	L	X	S	E	L	M	A	B	A	C	H	A	M

PAGE 45: NAME GAME

Federico Valverde — MID — POWER PLAY 76 — 6.5M — SHOOTING HERO — DEFENCE 78 — ATTACK 74 — LIMITED EDITION

Leroy Sane — MID — POWER PLAY 84 — 8.0M — DEFENCE 39 — ATTACK 84 — EMERALD LIMITED EDITION

Fred — MID — POWER PLAY 73 — 6.0M — DEFENCE 76 — ATTACK 68 — EMERALD LIMITED EDITION

Gabriel Jesus — FOR — POWER PLAY 79 — 7.5M — HAT-TRICK HERO — DEFENCE 32 — ATTACK 82 — LIMITED EDITION

PAGES 50–51: QUIZ: GOAL MACHINES

1 – **D:** Erling Haaland
2 – **B:** 2017
3 – **B:** Hat-trick
4 – **A:** Chloe Kelly
5 – **C:** 8
6 – **A:** Everton
7 – **C:** 36
8 – **C:** 7
9 – **C:** 141
10 – **C:** Arsenal

PAGES 60–61: QUIZ: FOOTY FIGURES

1 – 38
2 – 11
3 – 25
4 – 3.96 million
5 – 18
6 – 60,704
7 – 2,173
8 – 4-4-2
9 – 110
10 – 2